The Nature Kid's Guide to
FLYING SQUIRRELS

DAVID ANDERSON

LP Media Inc. Publishing
Text copyright © 2026 by LP Media Inc.
All rights reserved.

For information address LP Media Inc. Publishing,
30012 Variolite St NW, Princeton MN 55371
www.lpmedia.org

Publication Data

Flying Squirrels
The Nature Kid's Guide to Flying Squirrels — First edition.

Summary: "Learn all about Flying Squirrels, the Nature Kid Way"
— Provided by publisher.

ISBN: 979-8-89818-162-8

[1. Flying Squirrels – Non-Fiction] I. Title.

Title: The Nature Kid's Guide to Flying Squirrels

CONTENTS

BEYOND BACKYARDS

Whoosh! A flying squirrel leaps from a tree in the dark.

Flying squirrels live all over the world. You can find them on every continent except Australia and Antarctica. They are more common than you might think!

Most flying squirrels come out at night. They are nocturnal, so many people never see them. During the day, they rest in cozy tree holes.

There are about fifty kinds of flying squirrels. Some are tiny. Others are as big as a house cat! But they all share one cool trick. They can glide through the air like furry little kites.

GLIDING GREATNESS

Poof! A northern flying squirrel leaps off a branch and starts to glide.

Flying squirrels do not really fly. Only birds and bats can truly fly by flapping their wings. These furry animals glide from tree to tree instead.

Gliding means floating through the air without flapping. The squirrel jumps from up high, then sails down to a lower spot. It loses about three feet of height for every ten feet it travels forward.

People named them flying squirrels long ago. The name stuck even though it is not quite right. Gliding squirrels would be a much better name!

PATAGIUM POWER

Baby flying squirrels start practicing short glides when they are just six weeks old!

Pop! A southern flying squirrel glides and lands on a tree trunk.

Flying squirrels have a special body part called a **patagium**. Say it like this: puh-TAY-jee-um. It is a thin flap of fur-covered skin that connects each front leg to each back leg.

When the squirrel jumps, it spreads its legs wide. The skin stretches flat like a tiny cape. This catches the air and lets the squirrel glide smoothly between trees.

When a flying squirrel is not gliding, the skin folds up tight along its body. You might not even notice it is there! The patagium is like a hidden superpower.

GLIDING GLORY

Thump! A flying squirrel lands softly on the side of a tree.

Every glide starts at the top of a tall tree. The squirrel picks a landing spot, then leaps off the branch with its strong back legs. Whoosh!

The patagium catches the air like a kite. The squirrel steers by moving its legs and flat tail. It can turn left, right, or even slow down mid-flight.

Near the end, the squirrel lifts its body up. This acts like a brake for a soft landing. It grabs the trunk with all four feet and scurries around to the other side. This hides it from any owls watching from behind!

NIGHT EYES

FUN
FACT!
A flying squirrel's eyes are
so big that they cannot
move inside its head!

Scratch! A flying squirrel crawls out of its tree hole at dusk.

Flying squirrels come out at night. They are **nocturnal**, which means they sleep all day and wake up when darkness falls.

Their huge, round eyes help them see in dim light. Long whiskers help them feel things close by. These tools make them experts at moving through the dark forest.

Here is a wild secret. Flying squirrels glow bright pink under UV light! You cannot see this glow without a special lamp. Scientists discovered this surprise in 2019, and no one knows exactly why it happens.

SIZE SPECTRUM

14

Thud! A red and white giant flying squirrel lands on a thick jungle branch.

Flying squirrels come in many sizes. The smallest ones weigh less than an ounce. The biggest ones can weigh over three pounds!

Tiny flying squirrels are about five inches long. Giant ones stretch over three feet from nose to tail tip. That is a huge difference!

Bigger flying squirrels live in warm Asian forests. Smaller ones live in cooler places like Canada and Russia. Big or small, they are all amazing gliders built for life in the trees.

NORTHERN NAVIGATORS

Zip! A northern flying squirrel sits on a cold, snowy branch.

Northern flying squirrels live in cool forests across Canada and the northern United States. They love damp woods with big, old trees full of holes for nesting.

These squirrels eat nuts, seeds, and mushrooms. They also munch on tiny plants called lichens that grow on tree bark. When winter comes, they cuddle together in groups of up to twenty squirrels to stay warm.

Northern flying squirrels help the forest grow. They bury nuts and sometimes forget where they put them. Those lost nuts can sprout into new trees!

FUN FACT!

Up to fifty southern flying squirrels have been found sharing one winter nest!

Crunch! A southern flying squirrel nibbles an acorn on a limb.

Southern flying squirrels are one of the most common kinds in North America. They live in forests from Canada all the way down to Mexico and Central America.

These cute guys are a little bit smaller than their northern cousins. Most weigh only two to three ounces. They eat acorns, berries, bugs, and even bird eggs. They are not picky eaters at all!

Southern flying squirrels nest in old woodpecker holes. When forests are cut down, these squirrels lose their homes. Keeping old trees standing helps them survive for years to come.

SIBERIAN SOARING

DID YOU KNOW?

Siberian flying squirrels are the only flying squirrels found anywhere in Europe!

Fwip! A Siberian flying squirrel leaps from a birch tree trunk.

Siberian flying squirrels live in cold forests across Russia, China, and parts of northern Europe. They have soft, silvery-gray fur that keeps them warm in harsh winters.

These squirrels are small and very shy. They eat tree buds, seeds, and berries. In fall, they store extra food in tree holes for the long, dark winter ahead.

Siberian flying squirrels are losing some of their forest homes. People cut trees for wood and farms. Protecting old-growth forests helps these quiet gliders survive.

JAPANESE CUTIES

Japanese dwarf flying squirrels sometimes move into birdhouses to raise their babies!

Squeak! A tiny Japanese dwarf flying squirrel peeks from outside its nest.

Japanese dwarf flying squirrels live only in Japan. They make their homes in thick forests on cool, misty mountains.

These squirrels are tiny. One weighs only about 5-8 ounces! Their big, round eyes and fluffy fur make them look like living stuffed toys.

At night, they glide from branch to branch to find food. They eat tree buds, bark, and seeds. People in Japan love these little animals so much that they appear on stamps and in cartoons.

CRIMSON GLIDERS

Red and white giant flying squirrels make loud barking calls that echo through the forest at night!

Soar! A red and white giant flying squirrel glides through the forest!

Red and white giant flying squirrels live in parts of Asia. You can find them in China, India, and nearby mountain lands.

These squirrels are big. Really big! They can stretch over two feet long from nose to tail tip. Their fur is a striking mix of chestnut red and creamy white.

They spend most of their time high in tall trees, eating leaves, fruit, and pine cones after dark. Losing forest land is a serious threat to these colorful giants.

WOOLLY WONDER
DID YOU KNOW?
Woolly flying squirrels live more than 12,000 feet up — higher than many airplanes fly!
26

Swish! A woolly flying squirrel perches on a small cliff high up in the mountains.

Woolly flying squirrels live high in the mountains of Pakistan and China. They like rocky cliffs and thick, cold forests where few people ever go.

For many years, no one saw this squirrel. Scientists thought it might be extinct. Then in 1994, someone found one alive in the mountains of Pakistan! It was like finding a ghost.

These squirrels have thick, woolly fur to stay warm at high **altitudes**. They are among the biggest flying squirrels in the world. Protecting remote mountain forests keeps them safe.

SPOTTED SOARING
FUN FACT!
A spotted giant flying squirrel's fluffy tail can be as long as its entire body!
28

Whap! A spotted giant flying squirrel grips a tree with all fours.

Spotted giant flying squirrels live in forests across Southeast Asia. You can spot them in places like Vietnam, Thailand, and Indonesia.

Their dark fur has white or pale spots scattered across it. This pattern helps them hide in the dappled shadows of the forest at night. It is like wearing a built-in camouflage costume!

These big squirrels eat fruit, leaves, and nuts. They spend their nights high in the treetops, rarely coming to the ground. Cutting down their forest homes puts them in serious danger.

UNUSUAL TEETH

No other squirrel in the world has teeth quite like the complex-toothed flying squirrel!

Perch! A complex-toothed flying squirrel stands on a rocky cliff.

Complex-toothed flying squirrels live in mountain forests in China. They make their homes among rocky outcrops and ancient trees.

This squirrel gets its name from its unusual teeth. Its back teeth have many ridges and bumps, like tiny mountain ranges. These bumpy teeth help it crunch through tough bark and rock-hard seeds that other squirrels cannot eat.

These squirrels are rare and hard to find. Cutting down forests threatens their survival. Saving their mountain homes helps keep this unique species safe.

HORSFIELD'S GLIDER
DID YOU KNOW?
Horsfield's flying squirrel was first described by scientists way back in 1824!

Swoop! A Horsfield's flying squirrel climbs a branch in an Asian forest.

Horsfield's flying squirrels live in warm, tropical forests across Southeast Asia. They can be found in Malaysia, Java, Borneo, and many nearby islands.

This squirrel is named after Thomas Horsfield. He was a scientist who studied animals in Asia nearly 200 years ago. The squirrel has rich brown fur with a pale, creamy belly.

These squirrels eat fruit, leaves, and small insects. They need tall, thick forests to glide and find food. When people clear trees for farms, these gliders lose everything they need to survive.

ARROW
ACROBAT

DID YOU KNOW?

Arrow flying squirrels weigh only about three ounces — lighter than a deck of cards!

34

Zing! An arrow flying squirrel climbs between the jungle trees.

Arrow flying squirrels live in thick forests on islands across Southeast Asia. They got their name because they glide fast and straight, just like an arrow shot from a bow.

These squirrels are small and lightning quick. They have soft brown fur and a fluffy tail. At night, they zip from tree to tree through the dark jungle.

Arrow flying squirrels eat fruit, bugs, and sweet flower **nectar**. Keeping the island forests where they live safe is important for these speedy little gliders to thrive.

GLOWING GLIDERS
DID YOU KNOW?
Both male and female flying squirrels glow the exact same bright pink color!
36

Click! A UV lamp turns on and a flying squirrel glows bright pink.

In 2019, scientists shined a UV light on flying squirrels. Their fur lit up in a rosy pink glow! This discovery shocked the science world.

UV light is a kind of light human eyes cannot see. When it hits a flying squirrel's fur, something amazing happens. The fur soaks in the invisible light and gives off a soft pink glow instead.

Why do they glow? No one knows for sure yet. Maybe it helps them find each other in the dark. Maybe it confuses owls. Scientists are still working to solve this glowing mystery.

GLIDING GLOBALLY

Zoom! Flying squirrels glide across forests all around the world.

From tiny to giant, flying squirrels are full of surprises. These amazing gliders live in forests across Asia, Europe, and North America. About fifty different species call our planet home.

Some nest in snowy mountains. Some soar through steamy jungles. All of them glide through the trees at night using their stretchy skin flaps.

Flying squirrels need healthy forests to survive. We can help by protecting wild places and learning about these incredible animals. You just took the first step by reading this book!

GLOSSARY

patagium

A thin flap of skin that helps a flying squirrel glide

nocturnal

Active at night and sleeping during the day

hibernate

To enter a deep sleep through the cold winter

nectar

Sweet liquid found inside flowers

altitude

How high above sea level the ground is